Indoor Gardening Guide

How to successfully grow plants and vegetables inside your home, apartment, or office!

Table Of Contents

Introduction iv

Chapter 1 - Everything You Need to Know About Indoor Gardening 1

Chapter 2 - Choose Your Plants First 9

Chapter 3 - Designing a Container Garden 16

Chapter 4 - Designing a Hydroponic Garden 21

Chapter 5 - Preparing your Indoor Garden 24

Conclusion 26

Introduction

I want to thank you and congratulate you for downloading the book, *"Indoor Gardening Guide"*.

This book contains helpful information about indoor gardening, what it is, and everything you need to know to get started.

Indoor gardening can create an exciting space in your home, provide edible plants, and make all your friends envious of your living interior decorations.

Indoor plants are not only practical, they are attractive and are a great alternative if you don't have a large garden, or have mobility issues.

In the following chapters you will discover the differing ways in which you can construct an indoor garden, how to design your garden, what plants to grow, where to place your plants, and much, much more!

This book will explain to you tips and techniques that will help you successfully start your garden inside your home, office, or apartment! Good luck, I wish you the best with your gardening journey, and hope this book can be of some assistance to you.

Thanks again for downloading this book, I hope you enjoy it!

Chapter 1 - Everything You Need to Know About Indoor Gardening

Indoor gardening is all about what the name implies – gardening inside a home, office, or a building like a condo or apartment. It is popular among individuals who lack space for a usual garden and those who simply want to create a livelier interior for their home. It is also perfect for someone who wants to have fresh produce all the time even when the cold winter months arrive.

Understand that having an indoor garden takes more work than the typical garden, but the number of benefits that you will get is immense. You need to provide your plants with artificial lighting that replicates the rays of the sun. It needs more care than the outdoor garden. Take note that not all plants may be suitable for your indoor garden, but there are plants that are perfect for indoor gardening because they are easy to maintain under such an environment.

An indoor garden can provide a perfect interior decoration, its like capturing nature in a particular space. It can make the room practically breathe with the luscious greeneries, just make sure not to overdo it and turn your home into a jungle. It can give you fresh produce all-year round depending on the kind of plants that you want to have. It can filter the air in your home; there are plants that can also absorb formaldehyde in your furniture. There are also plants that can create a soothing and calming atmosphere and sensation, just what you need after a day of hard work.

Your Indoor Garden Set Up

Some people believe that placing a plant in a container and watering it everyday is all they need for their indoor garden. While there is some shade of truth in it, such practice will not make your indoor plants grow and last for long. Chances are, you will need to replace the plants time and again – that will prove to be more time consuming and expensive in the long run.

Wise planning can make you save time and money, and it can eliminate tons of headaches as well. Indoor gardening is only difficult at first, but once you are able to establish everything, it will become smooth from that point onwards.

The most important things that you need to consider in setting up an indoor garden are the kind of plants that you need (depending on the reason for having an indoor garden), the lighting, and set up (choose between soil or container garden and hydroponic). The supplies and materials are actually dependent on the three mentioned things. You will see a list of the things you require for different indoor gardens later in this chapter.

There are plants that require low maintenance and these are the most ideal for indoor garden. Your choice will also depend on your purpose of having an indoor garden – for added aesthetic appeal, having fresh produce all the time, or you simply want one because you don't have the luxury of space to do your gardening outside. There are lucky individuals who can grow any plants under any condition with so much ease and there are less fortunate ones who need to exert effort in making their indoor garden flourish. If you don't possess a green thumb, then it is best for you to choose the plants that are considered best for indoor use.

Not all indoor gardens rely on artificial lighting as their light source; there are buildings that can still provide the amount of natural sunlight needed for the indoor garden. If you want to utilize the natural lighting, then you need to set up your indoor garden near or directly in the area where your plants can get access to a natural light source. In most cases, artificial lighting is necessary to maintain the health and make your indoor garden grow. The artificial lighting may not be as good as the sun but it can help your indoor garden a lot.

You will also need to decide whether to choose soil (container garden) or hydroponics. Both types of indoor garden can benefit the indoor gardener; choose the one that you find more advantageous for your cause.

Things You Will Need

For a container or soil garden, you will need good compost (you can make your own although it may be difficult if you lack space), clean pots or containers, fertilizers, and potting mix.

For a hydroponic garden, you need a good hydroponic system which you can purchase from a store (local hydroponic store or garden supplies store) or you can build your own. If you are a novice gardener, it is best to have a store-bought system. You will also need containers – a big one or several small ones (size should be just right for a particular plant). You will also need perlite.

For either garden, you will need plants of your choice, a watering jug, thermometer, timers for controlling the lighting (only if you want to, otherwise do it manually), pesticide (in case an insect breakout occurs), oscillating fan (you can do without it, but it is best to have one), and ventilating system if you happen to grow plants with a strong smell. You can also choose to have white painted walls (or put white sheets on them) to make it more reflective.

For your artificial lighting, keep in mind that for every 18" x 18" garden patch, you need around 100 watts. You can also try CFL bulbs; they are a cheap option, otherwise ask your garden supplier for a cheap lighting that will do the job.

One of the many joys that indoor gardening can give (which outdoor gardening can't) is the controlled occurrence of pests. You can easily prevent the pests from invading your plants and your home by stopping them at once. You will be able to notice them immediately as compared to an outdoor garden which may take a while before you see the infestation.

Creating Your Own Compost and Compost Bin

Making your own compost is not costly and it is not difficult, but it could give off a strong smell if you are not too careful with the things you throw in. That is the reason why it is almost impossible to make your own compost if you lack space, but you can still choose to make your own compost and keep it inside your home. Remember to just throw in the things that will not attract pests or rodents, or give off a foul smell.

You can throw in trimmings or peelings of vegetables and fruits, tea bags, coffee grounds as well as filters, eggshells, cardboard, pieces of newspaper, grass clippings, paper, shells of nuts, leaves, yard trimmings, wood chips (sawdust included), cotton and wool rags, dead houseplants (without disease), hay, lint from dryer and vacuum cleaner, fur, hair, and ashes.

You should not throw in charcoal ash or coal, twigs or leaves of black walnut tree, dairy products (such as milk, yogurt, butter, egg white or yolk), fats (including lard, grease, and oil), meat scraps, fish bones, plants with disease, yard trimmings that were chemically treated, and pet wastes. The prohibited things may bring harm to you and your family members, invite pests, and give off a strong odor.

There are commercially available compost bins, but you can save more money if you create your own compost bin. Remember to look after your pile and keep track of the things that you put in the bin. A well managed compost bin will not let out an unpleasant odor and will not attract unwanted guests.

If you have an available plastic or metal container (with lid) at home that is big enough for the compost that you want to make, then all you need to do is drill or punch some holes (about half an inch in diameter) in the sides and bottom of the container. You also need a big enough tray to accommodate your compost bin. Line your tray with newspaper and put the bin on the tray. Inside the bin, add some dirt (about three inches deep or according to the amount of compost that you will need). Add some dry stuff like paper or shredded newspaper. Add the permitted materials in the bin.

You need to make sure that there is balance between the wet and dry components of the compost to avoid unpleasant smells. Mix or turn your compost at least once a week and you may need to add a bit of new soil occasionally. Your compost will be good to go in two to four weeks.

Useful Indoor Gardening Tips to Keep in Mind

In selecting containers for the plants, choose the ones that have proper drain holes or add holes to your containers to meet the ideal number of drain holes. Proper drainage can keep your plants out of harm's way.

People of different ages can benefit from catching the early morning rays of the sun, and the same goes with plants. Give your plants a dose of sunshine by moving them outside in the morning, and then get them back again before the sun's heat becomes intense.

Whenever you place your pots outside to catch some rays, see to it that your plants do not face the same direction each and every time. You need to rotate the position of the pots or make the plants face different directions each time you bring them out. There are plants that sway to where the sun is and they often grow inclined. To make sure that your plants will grow straight, make it a habit to turn them around.

A change in the color of the leaves may indicate presence of pests, inadequate light, or over watering. You can try removing the pests (that try to invade your plants) by hand or use a pesticide. If the leaves become darker than normal, then your plants need more light. If the natural green color of the leaves begin to turn yellow despite proper care and maintenance, then you are overwatering the plant. Make sure to pour only adequate water and do not go beyond the normal amount.

Feed your plants with fertilizers to maintain their health. You also need to spray water on the stem and leaves as if giving your plants a bath to remove the dust that makes them dull and appear lifeless.

Now that you have the basics, it is time to move on to the next step before deciding on the kind of set up that you want for your indoor garden.

Chapter 2 - Choose Your Plants First

If you really want to have an indoor garden but don't have the skills and confidence to grow a plant, then you need to choose the plants that are considered low maintenance and ideal for indoor gardening. You may also need to consider the kind of appeal that you want for a particular room in your house. Do you like flowering plants or fruit bearing ones? You may also opt to have some herbs and aromatic plants in your home. You can choose to have two to three of each kind, but be wary that you don't overcrowd your house with too many plants.

Fruits or Vegetables for Indoor Gardening

It is best to group the fruits and vegetables that love light together and those that are fine with partial light together. This way you will be able to give the correct amount of artificial light to each group separately.

Light lovers that are great for indoor gardening include tomato, eggplant, beans, okra, pepper, and cucumber.

Those that are fine with partial light are peas, carrot, lettuce, broccoli, spinach, scallions, cabbage, collard greens, beets, strawberries, blackberries, and raspberries.

Growing Your Fruits and Vegetables

If you plan to grow fruits and vegetables indoor, it is best to place each plant in a larger container (a 5-gallon container and up will suffice) to provide room to grow.

If you want to utilize the natural light of the sun, the ideal spot would be near the window that faces south, or alternatively the north if you are situated in the southern hemisphere. If you happen to have eastern window, then this is good too, but you may need to provide artificial lighting to ensure the proper growth of your fruits and vegetables.

Growing fruits and vegetables indoor requires human intervention in pollination. To achieve this, you need to gently shake the flowers or place a fan near the flowers to simulate the vibration or the wind that helps distribute the pollen.

Give the same care that you give the outdoor plants. During the absence of natural light in the day you need to turn the grow lights on. Turn it off when the sun sets.

If you have followed all the things correctly, then you will be harvesting your produce (depending on variety) in no time at all. Don't forget to give the correct nourishments that your plants need.

Growing Herbs and Aromatic Plants

A good selection of herbs for indoor gardening includes basil, oregano, parsley, thyme, rosemary, mint, jasmine, chives, sage, chamomile, and lavender.

It is best to place the herbs near the kitchen window and all you need to do is gather and add some to your dish. Aromatic plants are best for bedrooms because they can provide a soothing and relaxing scent that can calm the mind, body, and spirit. Jasmine is nice to put in the dining area to give a pleasant atmosphere while eating.

You can put each of these plants in individual small to medium containers that fit the size of the plant (unlike in fruit bearing plants).

Ornamental and Flowering Plants for Indoors

Ornamental and flowering plants can provide added aesthetic appeal to the interior of your home. There are also some that give added benefits aside from creating a different surrounding for the different rooms in your house such as your living, dining, recreation, and bedroom.

The snake plant or more popularly known as mother-in-law's tongue has spiked leaves of two to three feet long. This plant is not fond of water and the soil must be dry before watering it again. The good thing about this plant is that it is easy to maintain and can be a great addition to the interior of your home, just make sure not to over water it.

Devil's ivy can provide a different kind of atmosphere in the room. It is an attractive climbing plant that you can allow to hang or prepare a frame that it can climb.

Peace lily is a cute plant with white colored flowers that can provide a striking view. It can grow up to three feet and does not need to be watered frequently. It can help filter the toxins in the air, but it is advisable to keep children away from the leaves because it may harm them.

Jade plants need more sunlight and you may need to take them out during the day to catch some sun or make sure that they will be able to get the amount of light they need from the artificial source. They are regarded as good Feng Shui plants.

Dragon trees only need average care. They need to be placed in dry locations with the right amount of light. These plants are great for apartments and offices.

Chinese evergreen requires low maintenance, it is easy to grow, and definitely looks attractive in any space. It has leaves that measure on average one and a half feet long. It comes in different varieties with dark green leaves of different patterns.

Orchids never fail to attract undivided attention with their lovely flowers. Their presence alone is enough to exude romance in the air. Most varieties only need to be watered once a week. If the orchid has medium colored leaves, then you don't need to worry because it is normal, but if the leaves turn yellow it only means that you are overwatering the plant. It is best to buy orchids with buds that are ready to bloom.

Cast iron plant is one of the suitable plants for a novice indoor gardener. It is sturdy and requires low maintenance. It grows green colored leaves of around two feet long.

Spider plants filter the air off harmful elements like formaldehyde (in furniture) and carbon monoxide that can put your health at risk. It is good to have these plants around the house especially if you have younger children or are elderly.

Boston fern is another plant that can filter formaldehyde in the air surrounding your home and helps keep the air fresh and clean.

African violets are simply gorgeous and the best part is that they are easy to grow and maintain. They require less intense light so placing them in the eastern window is a good choice because they won't catch much sunlight. If your house has more windows and sunlight can penetrate the entire room, you can use curtains to block some of the sun's rays for your African violets.

Areca palm has the ability to clear the presence of xylene in the surroundings. Xylene can bring health risks when inhaled and it is present in most paints, pesticides, and gas. Areca palm can provide fresh and clean air all the time.

If you want to create a tropical feel in the room, then chamaedorea palm is the one to get.

Ponytail palms are beautiful and they don't require much attention. This plant is best for those indoor gardeners who don't have time to attend to their garden properly.

Sword ferns can tolerate dryness to an immense degree and most novice indoor gardeners may find this appealing. They provide great presence without asking so much in return.

Care and proper growing of these plants depend on the set up that you will be using.

Important Notes to Keep in Mind

An indoor garden is generally small, and there is a need to limit the number of plants to keep inside the house. Overcrowding is bad for your plants and your interior as well. Keep everything simple, organized, and neat. Avoid turning a particular space (or the whole house) into some kind of a messy forest.

If you are a novice gardener, it is best to start with hardy and disease-resistant varieties of indoor garden plants.

Since there are no natural pollinators inside the house, it is best to pollinate flowers using small brush as well as the suggestions already mentioned.

Neem oil can limit indoor diseases and pests when you spray some on the leaves and stems of the plants. The oil acts as a natural pesticide, fungicide, and discourages the feeding of insects. Neem oil is completely safe to use and neem is also popular in treating various ailments in humans.

It is best to get rid of the plants or remove the leaves that show signs of a disease or mold. Not doing anything about it may infect other healthy indoor plants.

If you have decided to use fish in your hydroponic set up, it is advisable to put fish in the tank seven days after you have installed your hydroponic system.

If you already have the plants for your indoor garden, then the next thing to do is decide whether to have a container garden or a hydroponic garden. Either set up is good and all you need is to choose the one that best suits your preference.

Chapter 3 - Designing a Container Garden

Designing a container garden is not difficult to do. You can have hanging, wall mounted, or the usual arrangement. You need proper planning (and enormous creativity) in order to have a great looking indoor garden.

The Right Containers

In designing a container garden, it is advisable to choose your containers wisely. You can use different containers but keep in mind to choose larger containers for growing fruits and vegetables. You can use traditional pots and vases, plastic bottles, bucket, different containers from a garden supply shop, or make your own. Remember to have enough holes to provide proper drainage for the plants.

Plastic containers can effectively retain moisture, but terra cotta pots can give added beauty to the whole garden.

For herbs and smaller plants, you can recycle coffee cans or plastic bottles and create a true green garden. Never recycle containers that have been used for chemicals or have been treated with chemicals, the chemical residue may kill your plants.

If you use a wooden container, then make sure to pick rot resistant wood like cedar or redwood.

After choosing the right containers for your plants you can now line the bottom of each container with rocks or stones for added drainage.

The Potting Mix

Even though the soil that can be found outside your home may be used for your indoor garden, it is not safe. Most of the time, the soil from outside has disease and unknown insects that might kill your plants later. You can purchase a prepared potting mix from a garden supply store if you don't have time to make one.

The ideal potting mix is one part each of vermiculite and coir peat, and two parts compost (it is best to start composting first at least weeks before the intended indoor garden is set up). You can buy all of the said materials from a local garden supplier and you will save some money if you will use your own compost.

Soak the coir peat in water to start the rehydration process. It usually comes with instructions regarding soaking and all you need to do is follow the procedure.

Mix the coir peat and vermiculite together and make sure to mix it well before adding the compost. If you can, try adding worm castings to the mixture (about half cup to a cup) because worm castings can give added benefits to the plants.

Setting Up Your Container Garden

Now that everything is ready, you have to decide on the right spot to put your indoor garden. You need to determine the amount of light that can enter the room. It should be an ideal area where you can install your artificial lighting, temperature, and water system without trouble. If you plan to have a large garden inside your home, it is crucial to have a shelving system for your plants. If you have shelving system, you simply hang the drip system and artificial lights to the shelves. Otherwise, you will need to spend extra hours of work getting all the components adjusted.

You can set up timers for your artificial lights and drip system. Leave it on during crucial times within the day when your plants need it.

As mentioned earlier, there are plants that are fond of sunlight and there are plants that don't like light that much. It is important to group together the plants that love light and the plants that like partial light so that each group will only get the right amount of needed light when the artificial lights are on.

Proper Maintenance of the Plants

Proper maintenance is of utmost importance, that's why there is a need for you to choose the plants first before proceeding with the project. Make sure that your plants get the right amount of light and the soil temperature should not go below 70°F.

When your plants begin to crowd, you need to transfer the plants to a bigger container or divide the plants with the purpose of keeping the plants to yourself or to be distributed as gifts to friends and family.

Browning or wilting leaves look unappealing and it may indicate that the plant has a disease. It is best to remove the infected plant from the garden and save yourself some trouble.

Add compost or fertilizers every few months to make sure that your plants get adequate nutrients.

Some Creative Ideas for Container Gardens

There are some indoor gardeners who prefer to hang their garden and some have upside down herbs ready for the picking. The containers used to achieve such effect have protective guards to prevent the plant and soil from falling. Some have hanging containers with unique designs.

You can also create a wall full of plants by mounting the containers or have a built in open shelf where you can put your indoor garden. The design of the wall is only limited by your imagination. You can even decorate it with minute wall climbers and create a world with a different kind of adventure.

You can also build a moving frame for your plants that allows you to move your plants anywhere in your house. You can even bring your plants out by pushing the frame out of the house and let your plants feast on the warm rays of the sun.

There are still unexplored ideas for indoor container gardens, and you might just stumble upon some great designs one day with some help from your imaginative mind.

If you want more information on container gardening, I have a book entirely devoted to this concept. Have a look at the other books by myself, Steve Ryan, to check it out!

Chapter 4 - Designing a Hydroponic Garden

There are several ways to set up your hydroponic garden, but they all have the same theme to follow: water tank at the bottom and plants as well as stacks of shelves on top.

How Hydroponics Works

The fertilized water coming from the tank is distributed or fed to the plants. You don't use the usual potting soil for hydroponic, you need to use perlite instead. The water is absorbed by the plants and the excess is drained back to the tank.

Some use fish to naturally fertilize the water. The fish waste and water create an ideal mixture to be fed to the plants. This combination of hydroponic gardening, and growing fish is known as aquaponics.

Small Scale or Large Scale Hydroponic System

If you intend to have a small scale hydroponic garden, then you don't have to prepare an enormous shelving unit and other supplies just to create the basic system. You can use plastic bottles (cut according to the size you need) and a window facing the sun. You can set up your hydroponic near the window and get adequate light.

For a large scale set up, it is best to use one large container instead of several small ones. You can also use a large tub to harvest lots of the same crop. Most indoor gardeners who prefer vegetables tend to prefer hydroponics.

Location is Important

A hydroponic garden also needs adequate light to make the plants grow, but in the absence of natural light it is best to set up the hydroponic garden with lots of vertical space for the shelving in order to properly support an artificial lighting system.

Take note that you should not put the shelves directly on top or under an air duct or air vent.

As much as possible, arrange your hydroponic garden on hard floors and not on carpeted one to prevent mildew and mold from occurring.

Preparing the Important Containers

Like in soil or container gardening, you also need to drill or punch holes on the containers that you are going to use for your hydroponic garden, if the containers don't have holes or if there are an inadequate number of holes.

Instead of the usual potting soil that you can use in a container garden, you need to use perlite in hydroponic gardens. Perlite is a porous soil replacement that is most suitable to use for this kind of garden. Plant your seeds accordingly and water them heavily to reduce or alleviate the shock from transplanting.

The System Set Up

Commercially available hydroponic systems usually come with easy to follow set up instructions – just follow the directions. If you are making your own set up, it is best to put the water tank at the bottom shelf that should be elevated (some inches above the ground).

Put your plant container or containers on the shelves and make sure that the containers are above the tank. There should not be too much space between the tank and the containers. Set up your pump system responsible for delivering water to the plants above the tank.

The artificial lighting (in the absence of natural light) should hang above the plants. You can set up a timer to save electricity.

You can also ask your local hydroponic expert (or where you purchased your system) for some advice regarding the set up if instructions are somewhat confusing.

Proper Maintenance of the System

Schedule a regular maintenance check for your system to make sure that it won't cause problems for you and your plants. Replenish the water in the tank if needed and make necessary adjustments as your plants grow. If you are using fish in your tank, see to it that each fish is in good health, fed properly, and has enough room to swim.

Water and electronics is a dangerous combination, it is best to hire an expert to do the wiring for you, just to make sure that nothing will go wrong in the long run.

Chapter 5 - Preparing your Indoor Garden

Now that you have the plants for your indoor garden, you know the set up to take, and other pertinent things to consider prior to the actual set up of your indoor garden, it's time to prepare your indoor garden.

The Preparation

The style or how your garden will look like solely depends on you. You may add artificial plants or other decorations to complement your garden. You can have a bit of aromatic, ornamental, flowering, and fruit bearing plants as well as herbs and vegetables – but make sure that they are organized and won't make your home look like a jungle model. You can also opt to have both set ups – the container garden and the hydroponic garden, provided that they will create harmony and do not clash.

Don't mix container garden and hydroponic gardens together. You need to set an area for your container garden and a separate area for your hydroponic, or you can choose only one set up (it is also more practical).

If you have a theme in mind, it is best to stick with the theme and aim to make your guests admire and envy your indoor garden.

The space for your indoor garden should be appropriate for the plants and concept of your garden. Choosing a random space to place your indoor garden may turn out to be unfavorable and awkward for the plants and the entire interior design of your home. Try to create a general look that you want to achieve with your chosen plants and set up.

Keep the right soil temperature all the time to ensure proper growth of your plants and to keep them healthy. Make sure that the room where your plants thrive has the correct temperature and moisture too.

Once everything has been settled, you can finally have an indoor garden that you can be proud of. Your indoor garden will definitely return the favor a thousand folds as thanks for the love and care that you have provided. Treasure your indoor garden and reap its many benefits and advantages.

Conclusion

Thank you again for downloading this book!

I hope this book was able to help you learn more about indoor gardening.

The next step is to put this information to use, and begin growing your indoor garden!

Remember to plan carefully, and don't overcrowd the space!

Also, don't forget to check out some of my other gardening books, I have plenty of them on a range of gardening styles!

Also, don't forget to claim your FREE bonus e-book on how to grow tomatoes!
Download your copy at the link below:

http://bit.ly/1ODGQbJ

Finally, if you enjoyed this book, please take the time to share your thoughts and post a review on Amazon. It'd be greatly appreciated!

Thank you and good luck!

www.ingramcontent.com/pod-product-compliance
Lightning Source LLC
LaVergne TN
LVHW021747060526
838200LV00052B/3515